How the Bear Lost His Tail

by Kate Pistone
illustrated by Hector Borlasca

Bear liked to eat.
In the spring, Bear
had fish to eat.

In the summer, Bear
had berries to eat.

In the fall, Bear
had honey to eat.

In the winter, it got cold.
Bear did not have fish, berries,
or honey to eat.

"Fox," said Bear,
"I can not get fish.
The lake is hard with ice.
There are no berries.
There is no honey.
What can I eat?"

"Let me help you," said Fox.
Fox liked to play tricks.
Fox went to his den
and got a fish.

"How did you get
a fish?" said Bear.

Fox made up a story to tell
Bear. "Look! I cut a hole in
the ice," said Fox. "I put my
tail in the hole and I got
a fish!"

"You can dig a hole, too! You can put your tail in the ice," said Fox.
So Bear dug a hole in the ice.

Bear put his tail in the hole. His tail was so cold. But he sat and sat.

Fox said, "Stand up, Bear. Did you get a fish?"

Bear said, "I can not stand. I am stuck. My tail has turned to ice!"

13

"I tricked you," said Fox,
and he ran.

Bear tugged and tugged
on his icy tail.
Bear got up.
But his tail was gone.

And that is how
Bear lost his tail!